BALTIMORE
ORIOLES
STARS, STATS, HISTORY, AND MORE!
BY K. C. KELLEY

The Child's World®
childsworld.com

Published by The Child's World®
1980 Lookout Drive • Mankato, MN 56003-1705
800-599-READ • www.childsworld.com

ISBN 9781503828162
LCCN 2018944829

Printed in the United States of America
PAO2392

Photo Credits:
Cover: AP Images/Patrick Semansky; Joe Robbins (inset).
Interior: AP Images: 9, Julie Jacobson 10, Roberto Birea
17, David Durochik 23; Dreamstime.com: Brandon Vincent
13; Newscom: Mark Goldman/Icon SMI 5, Mitch Stringer/
Icon SMI 20, Cliff Welch/Icon SMI 27, 29; Joe Robbins 6,
14, 24.

About the Author

K.C. Kelley is a huge sports
fan who has written more
than 100 books for kids. His
favorite sport is baseball.
He has also written about
football, basketball, soccer,
and even auto racing! He lives
in Santa Barbara, California.

On the Cover

Main photo: Infielder Tim Beckham;
Inset: Hall of Famer Cal Ripken Jr.

CONTENTS

GO, ORIOLES!

The Baltimore Orioles have a long history. The team was great in the 1970s. The Orioles have had some other good seasons, too. However, their fans have waited since 1983 for another **World Series** win. Will the Orioles be flying high again soon? Let's meet the O's!

Infielder Tim Beckham hopes to lead the Orioles back to the top! ➤

4

WHO ARE THE ORIOLES?

The Orioles play in the American League (AL). That group is part of Major League Baseball (MLB). MLB also includes the National League (NL). There are 30 teams in MLB. The winner of the AL plays the winner of the NL in the World Series.

◄ *Mark Trumbo is a home run hero for Baltimore fans.*

WHERE THEY CAME FROM

Today's Orioles began in 1894 as the Milwaukee Brewers. That's a different team than today's Milwaukee Brewers! In 1902, the early Brewers moved to St. Louis. The team became the Browns. From 1902 to 1953, the Browns were in only one World Series! In 1954, the team moved to Baltimore. The team was re-named after the Maryland state bird.

Hall of Fame player Rogers Hornsby ➤ managed the Browns for six seasons.

WHO THEY PLAY

The Orioles play in the AL East Division. The other teams in the AL East are the Boston Red Sox, the New York Yankees, the Tampa Bay Rays, and the Toronto Blue Jays. The Orioles play more games against their division **rivals** than against other teams. In all, the Orioles play 162 games each season. They play 81 games at home and 81 on the road.

◄ *Got him! The Orioles catcher tags out a Yankees runner.*

WHERE THEY PLAY

The Orioles moved into Oriole Park at Camden Yards in 1992. It was a beautiful new ballpark. It reminded fans of old-time stadiums. More than a dozen other teams saw what the Orioles had done. Then they made their own new ballparks, too! Camden Yards is still a great place to play. A huge brick building stands behind right field. Fans have a great view of Baltimore Harbor nearby.

Oriole Park at Camden Yards uses a lot of brick for an old-time feeling. ➤

OUTFIELD

FOUL LINE

THIRD BASE ▼

COACH'S BOX ▲

THE BASEBALL FIELD

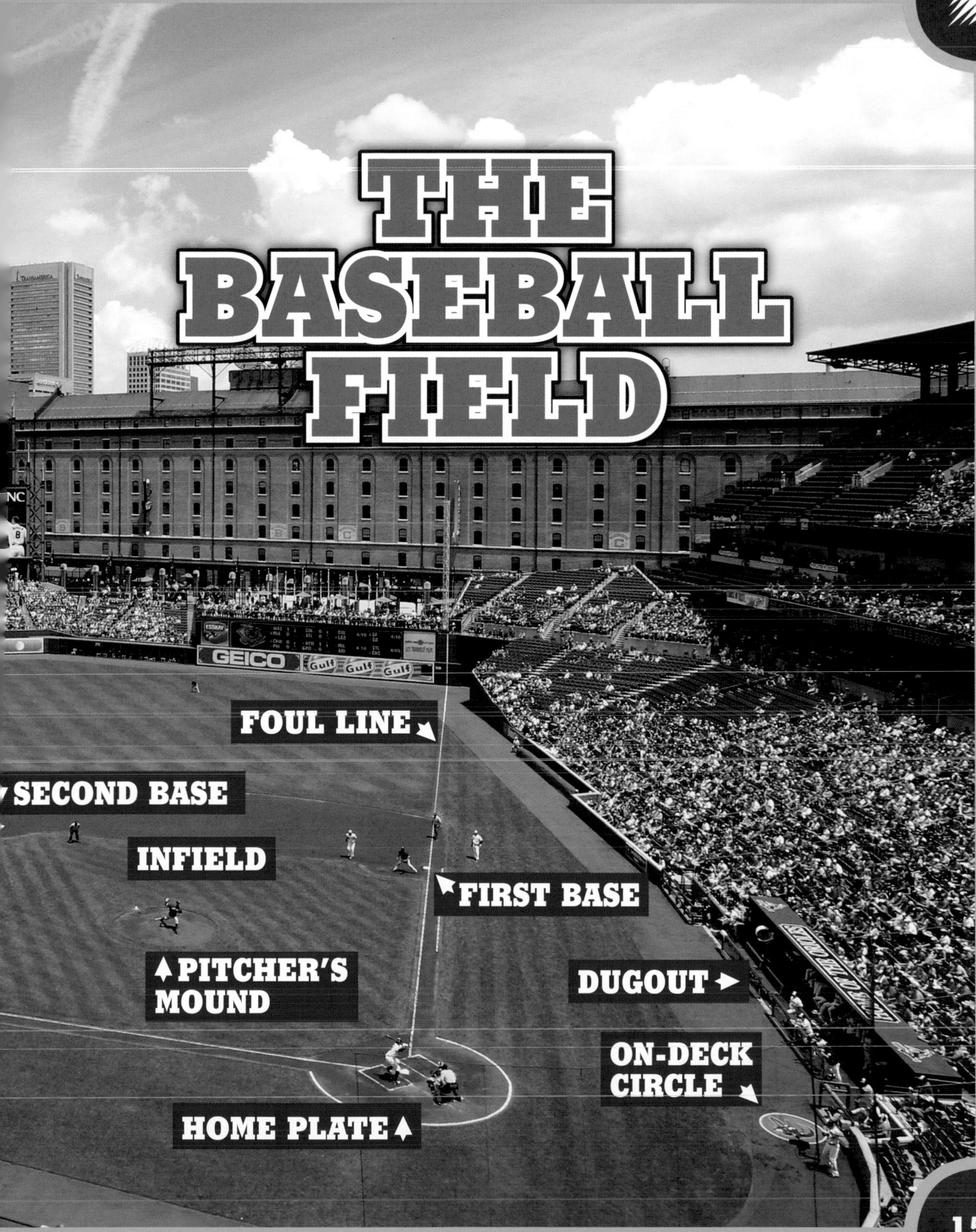

FOUL LINE

SECOND BASE

INFIELD

FIRST BASE

PITCHER'S MOUND

DUGOUT

ON-DECK CIRCLE

HOME PLATE

BIG DAYS

The Orioles have had a lot of great days in their long history. Here are a few of them.

1966—After many years of losing, the Orioles finished on top! They won their first World Series by beating the Los Angeles Dodgers.

1983—Shortstop Cal Ripken Jr. helped the O's win their third World Series. They beat the Philadelphia Phillies.

1995—Ripken set a new baseball record. He played in his 2,131st straight game. He later finished his amazing streak of playing 2,632 games without missing one.

Cal Riplen Jr. was honored here when he tied the all-time record ➤
for games played in a row. He broke the record the next night.

TOUGH DAYS

Like every team, the Orioles have had some not-so-great days, too. Here are a few their fans might not want to recall.

1939—As the Browns, the team had a lot of bad seasons. The worst came this year. The Browns lost a club-record 111 games. (That record was later topped by the 2018 Orioles. The O's lost 115 games!)

1988—Talk about bad starts! The O's lost their first 21 games! That was the worst start by a team ever. Baltimore ended the season with 107 losses.

1991—Wilson Alvarez of the Chicago White Sox was making only his second start in MLB. The young pitcher threw a surprise **no-hitter** against the Orioles!

▼ *Cal Ripken's brother Billy tried to make this play in 1988. Like most things that year, it didn't work.*

MEET THE FANS!

Orioles fans are very loyal. They stick with their team through thick and thin. At games, they get help cheering from the Oriole Bird. It's the team's **mascot**. Baltimore fans are also famous for singing. During the **National Anthem**, they loudly yell "O!" when they hear "O say can you see . . ." Can you guess why they do that?

◄ *The Oriole Bird tries out as a pitcher!*

HEROES THEN

Many great players have worn the Orioles orange and black. Brooks Robinson was probably the best-fielding third baseman ever. Frank Robinson was a **slugger** who won the AL Most Valuable Player Award. Eddie Murray was a great hitter from both sides of the plate. Pitcher Jim Palmer had eight seasons with 20 or more wins. Cal Ripken Jr. set the games-played streak. He was also a 19-time All-Star!

Frank Robinson helped the Orioles win the 1970 World Series. ➤

23

HEROES NOW

Adam Jones is the Orioles biggest star. He's a hard-hitting outfielder. Tim Beckham has good power at third base. Trey Mancini looks like he could become a home run hero. Dylan Bundy is Baltimore's top starting pitcher. Andrew Cashner could become another solid pitcher in Baltimore.

◄ *Trey Mancini had 24 homers in 2017, his first full season with the O's.*

GEARING UP

Baseball players wear team uniforms. On defense, they wear leather gloves to catch the ball. As batters, they wear hard helmets. This protects them from pitches. Batters hit the ball with long wood bats. Each player chooses his own size of bat. Catchers have the toughest job. They wear a lot of protection.

THE BASEBALL

The outside of the Major League baseball is made from cow leather. Two leather pieces shaped like 8s are stitched together. There are 108 stitches of red thread. These stitches help players grip the ball. Inside, the ball has a small center of cork and rubber. Hundreds of feet of yarn are tightly wound around this center.

CATCHER'S MASK AND HELMET

CHEST PROTECTOR →

WRIST BANDS

CATCHER'S MITT

SHIN GUARDS

CATCHER'S GEAR

TEAM STATS

Here are some of the all-time career records for the Baltimore Orioles. All these stats are through the 2018 regular season.

HOME RUNS

Cal Ripken Jr.	431
Eddie Murray	343

RBI

Cal Ripken Jr.	1,695
Brooks Robinson	1,357

BATTING AVERAGE

Henry Manush	.362
George Sisler	.344

STOLEN BASES

George Sisler	351
Brady Anderson	307

WINS

Jim Palmer	268
Dave McNally	181

SAVES

Gregg Olson	160
Zach Britton	139

Jim Palmer is the top pitcher in Orioles history. ➤

STRIKEOUTS

Jim Palmer	2,212
Mike Mussina	1,535

GLOSSARY

mascot (MASS-cot) a costumed character who helps fans cheer

National Anthem (NASH-un-ull ANN-thehm) "The Star-Spangled Banner," the official song of the United States, played before every MLB game

no-hitter (no-HIT-er) a game in which the starting pitcher wins and does not allow a hit to the other team

rivals (RYE-vuhlz) two people or groups competing for the same thing

slugger (SLUG-ger) a batter who hits a lot of home runs and extra-base hits

World Series (WURLD SEE-reez) the annual championship of Major League Baseball

FIND OUT MORE

IN THE LIBRARY

Connery-Boyd, Peg. *Baltimore Orioles: The Big Book of Activities*. Chicago, IL: Sourcebooks, Jabberwocky, 2016.

Smolka, Bo. *12 Reasons to Love the Baltimore Orioles*. Mankato, MN: 12-Story Library, 2016.

Sports Illustrated Kids (editors). *The Big Book of Who: Baseball*. New York, NY: Sports Illustrated Kids, 2017.

ON THE WEB

Visit our website for links about the Baltimore Orioles:
childsworld.com/links

Note to Parents, Teachers, and Librarians: We routinely verify our web links to make sure they are safe and active sites. So encourage your readers to check them out!

INDEX